CLARA CHLAMYDIA

LET'S COLOR
STDs

SEXUALLY TRANSMITTED DISEASES
ADULT COLORING BOOK

CLARA CHLAMYDIA

LET'S COLOR
STDs

SEXUALLY TRANSMITTED DISEASES
ADULT COLORING BOOK

Bibliografische Information der Deutschen Nationalbibliothek:
Die Deutsche Nationalbibliothek verzeichnet diese Publikation in
der Deutschen Nationalbibliografie; detaillierte bibliografische
Daten sind im Internet über http://dnb.dnb.de abrufbar.

(c) 2018 Clara Chlamydia
Herstellung und Verlag:
BoD – Books on Demand, Norderstedt
ISBN: 978-3-7528-2082-9

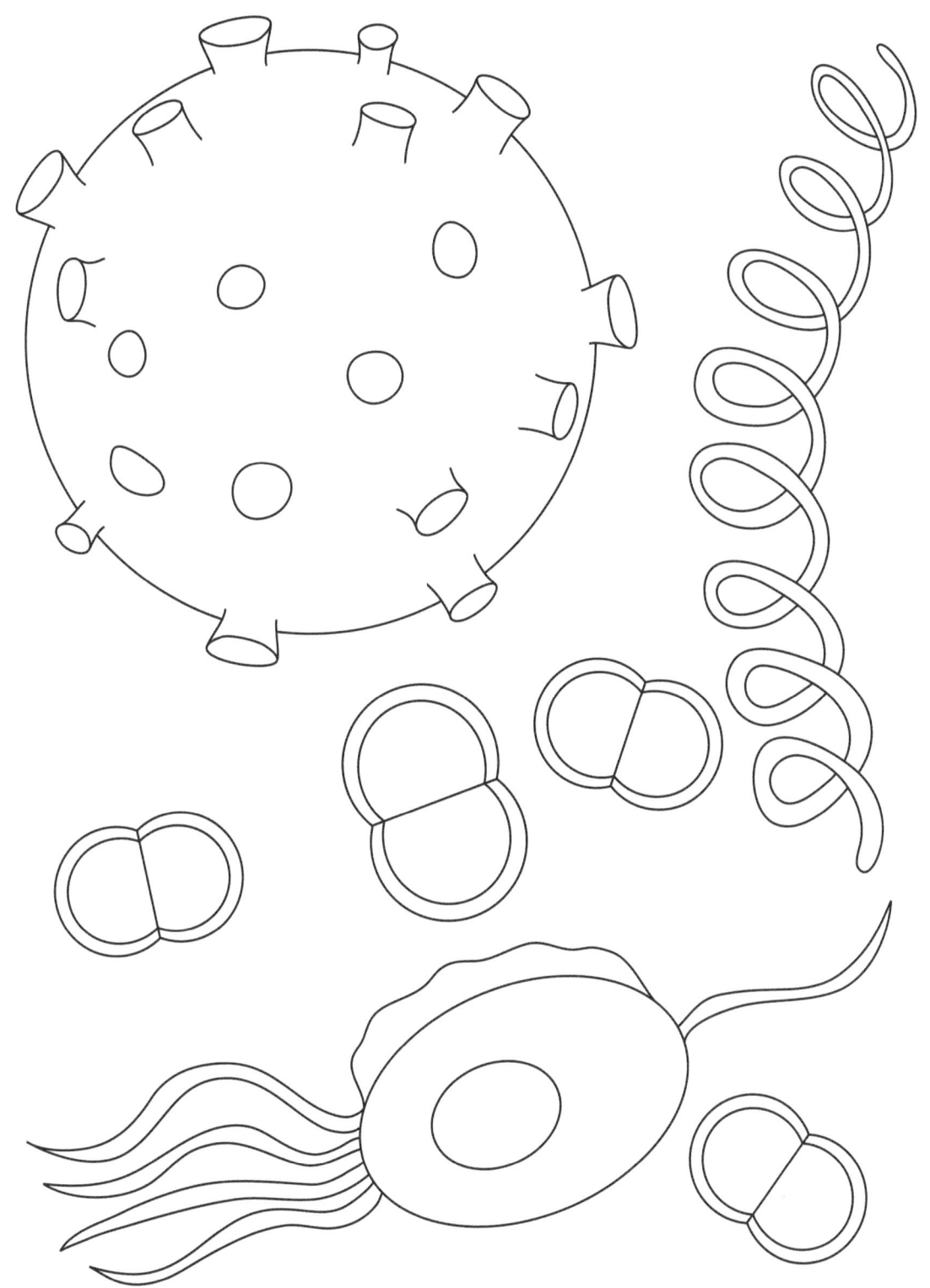

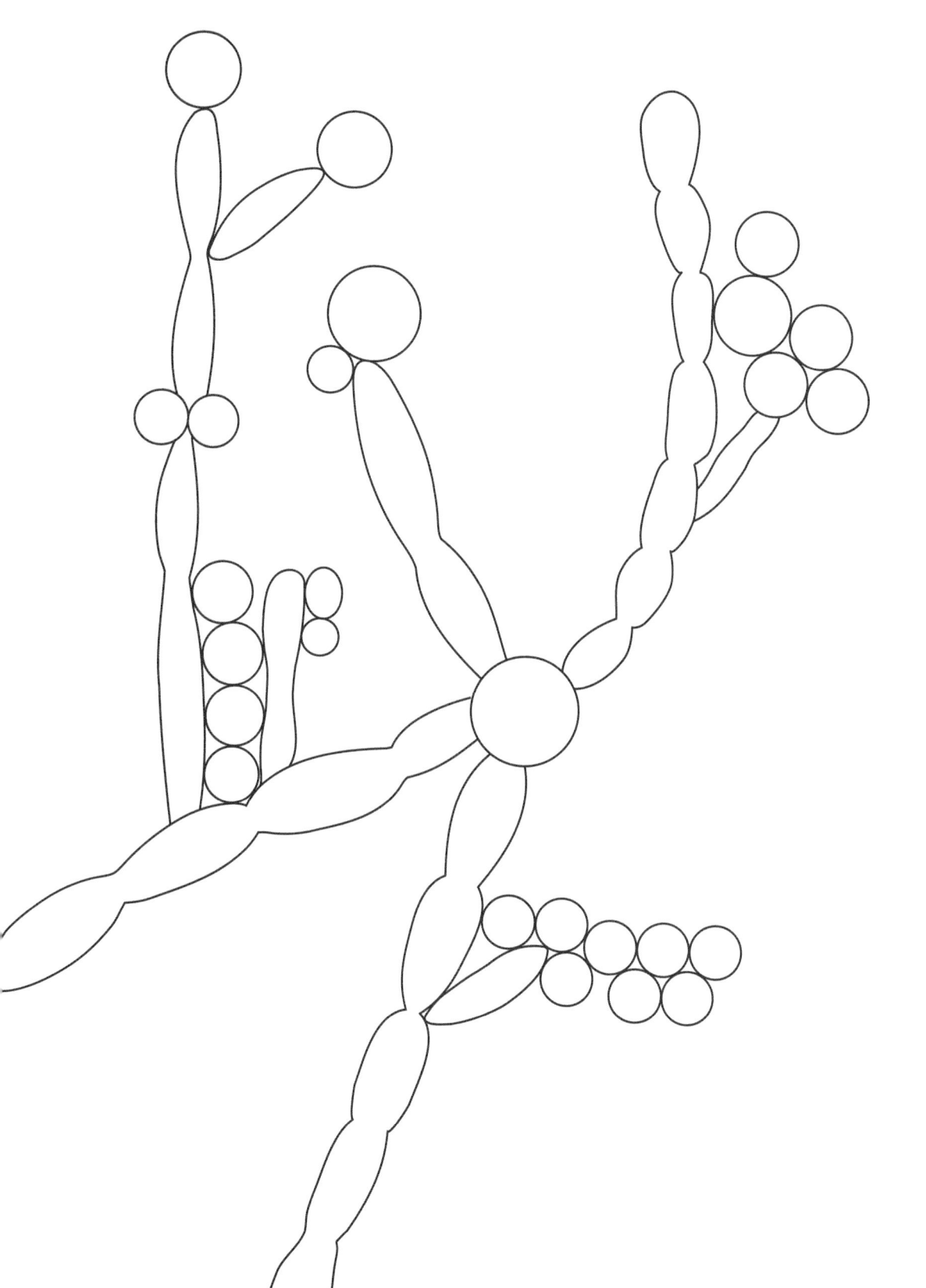

CHLAMYDIA➡

HEPATITIS B➡

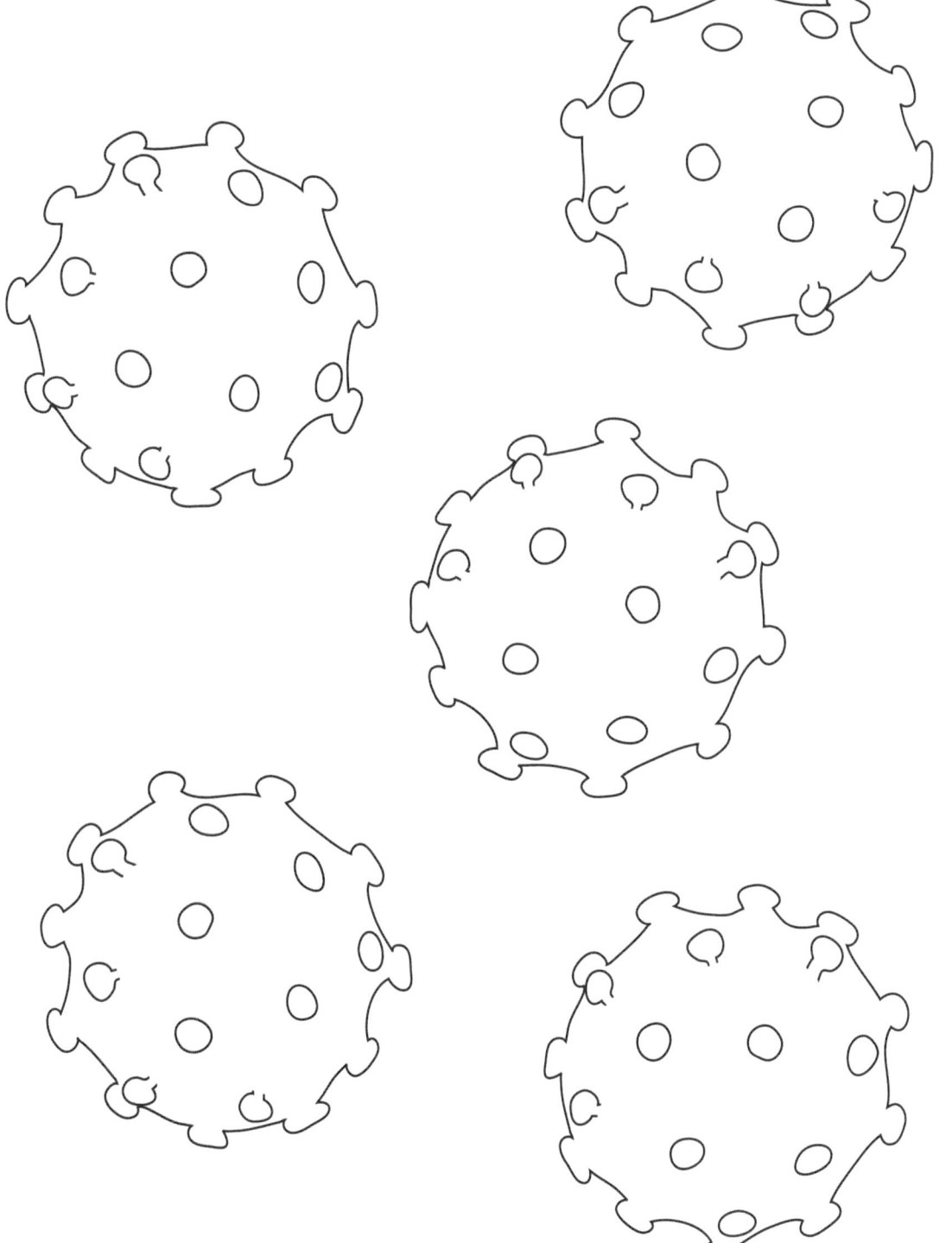

HERPES➡

HIV➡

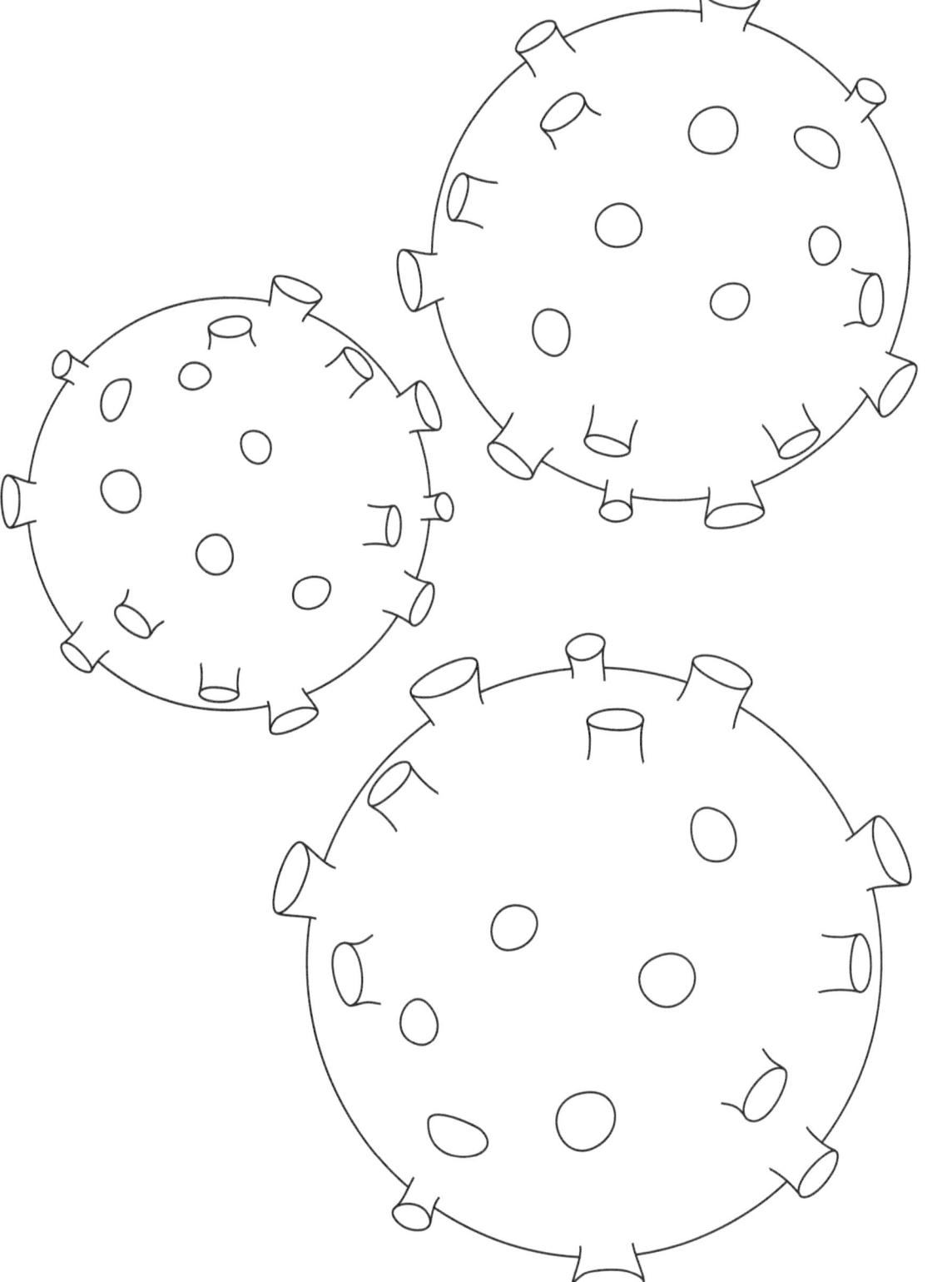

GONORRHEA➡

GENITAL WARTS➡

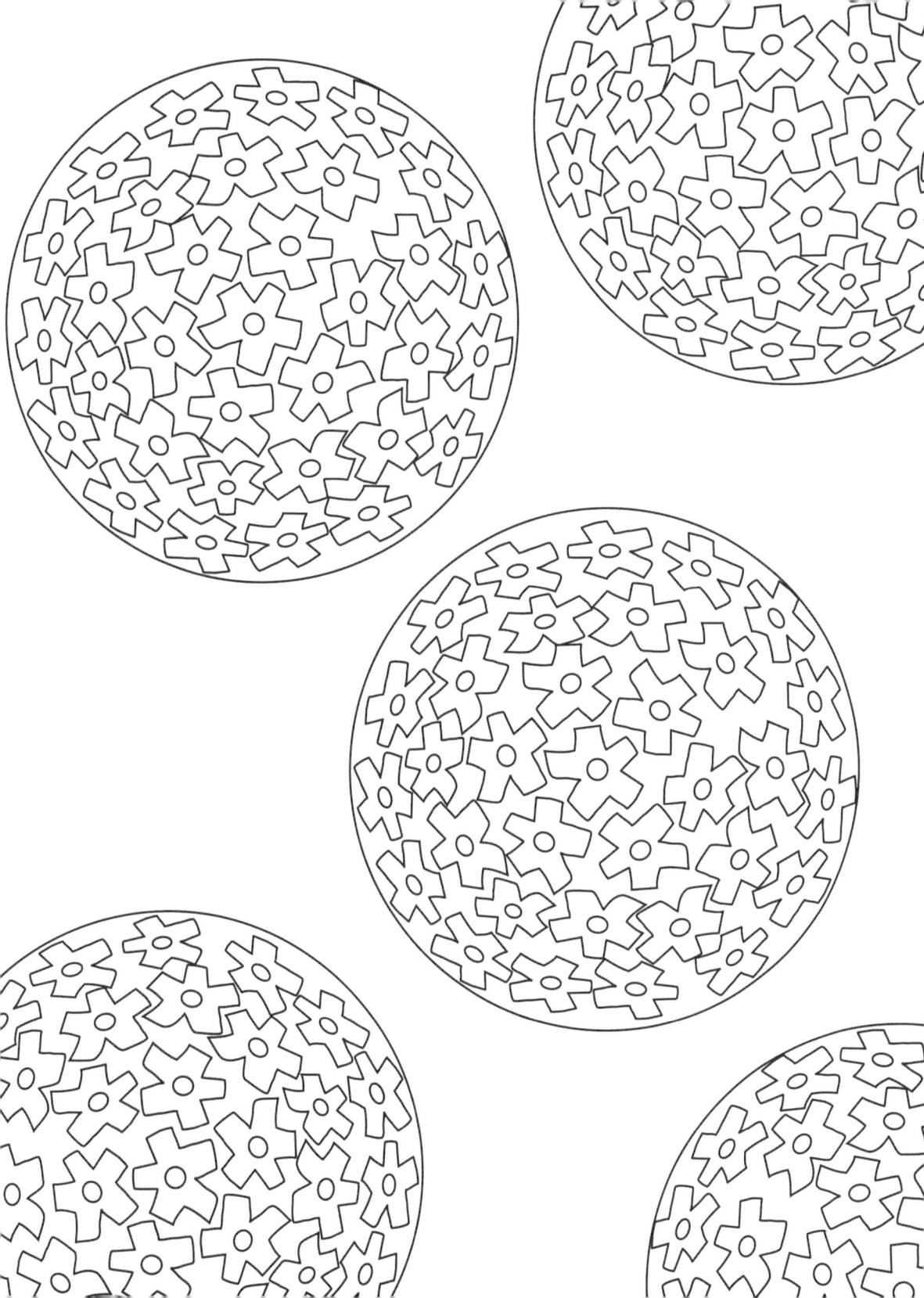

CHLAMYDIA➡

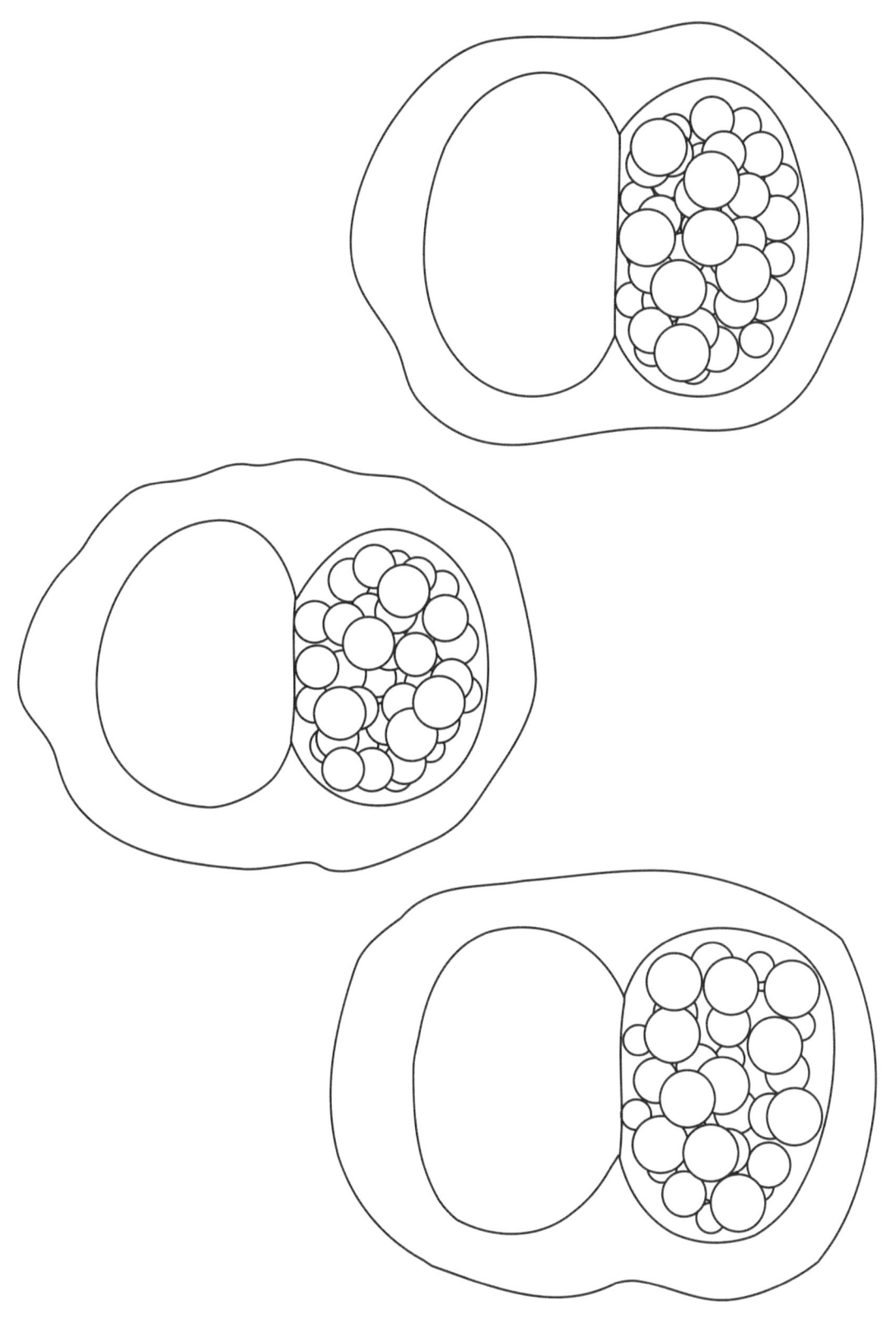

HERPES➡

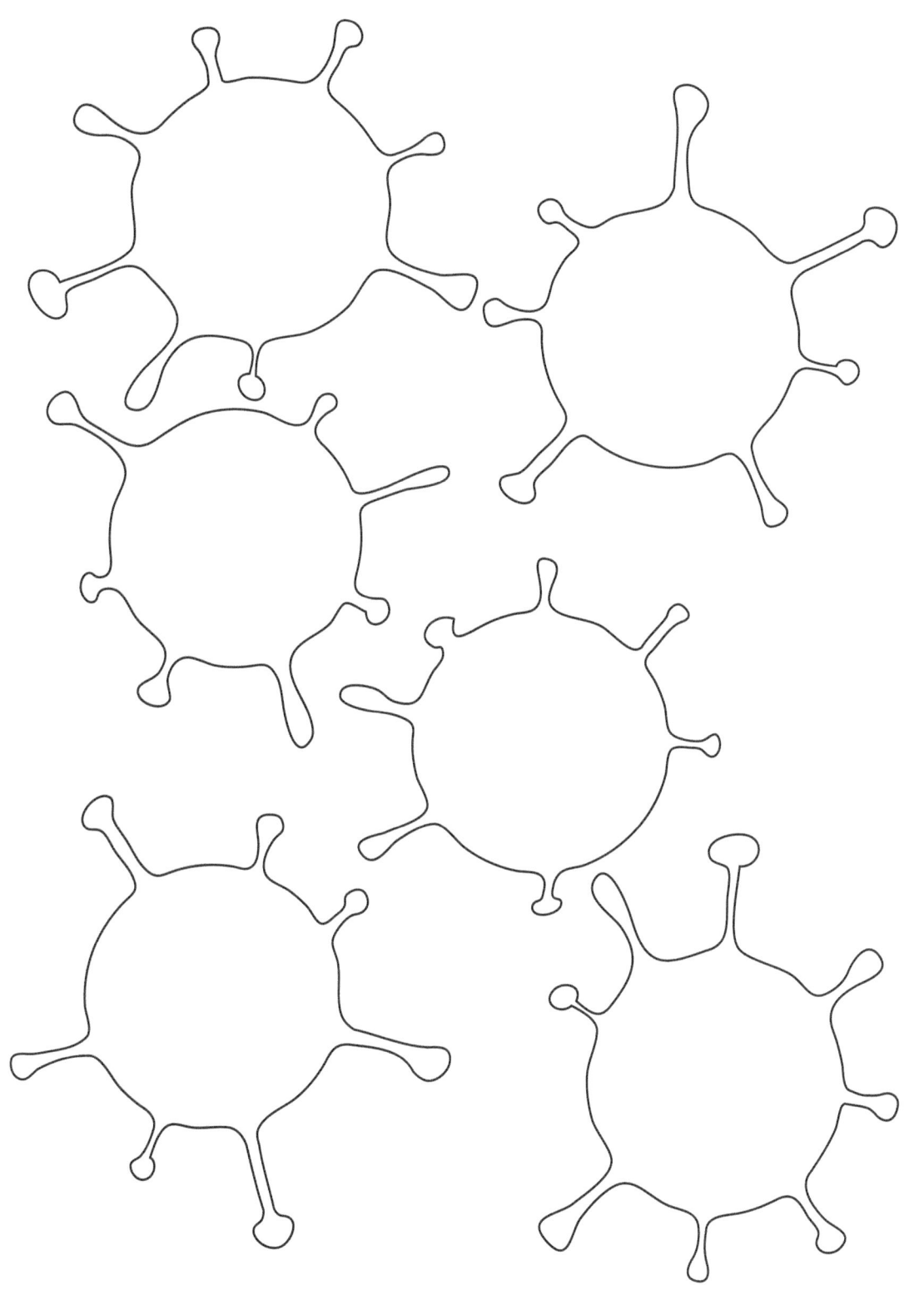

SYPHILIS➡

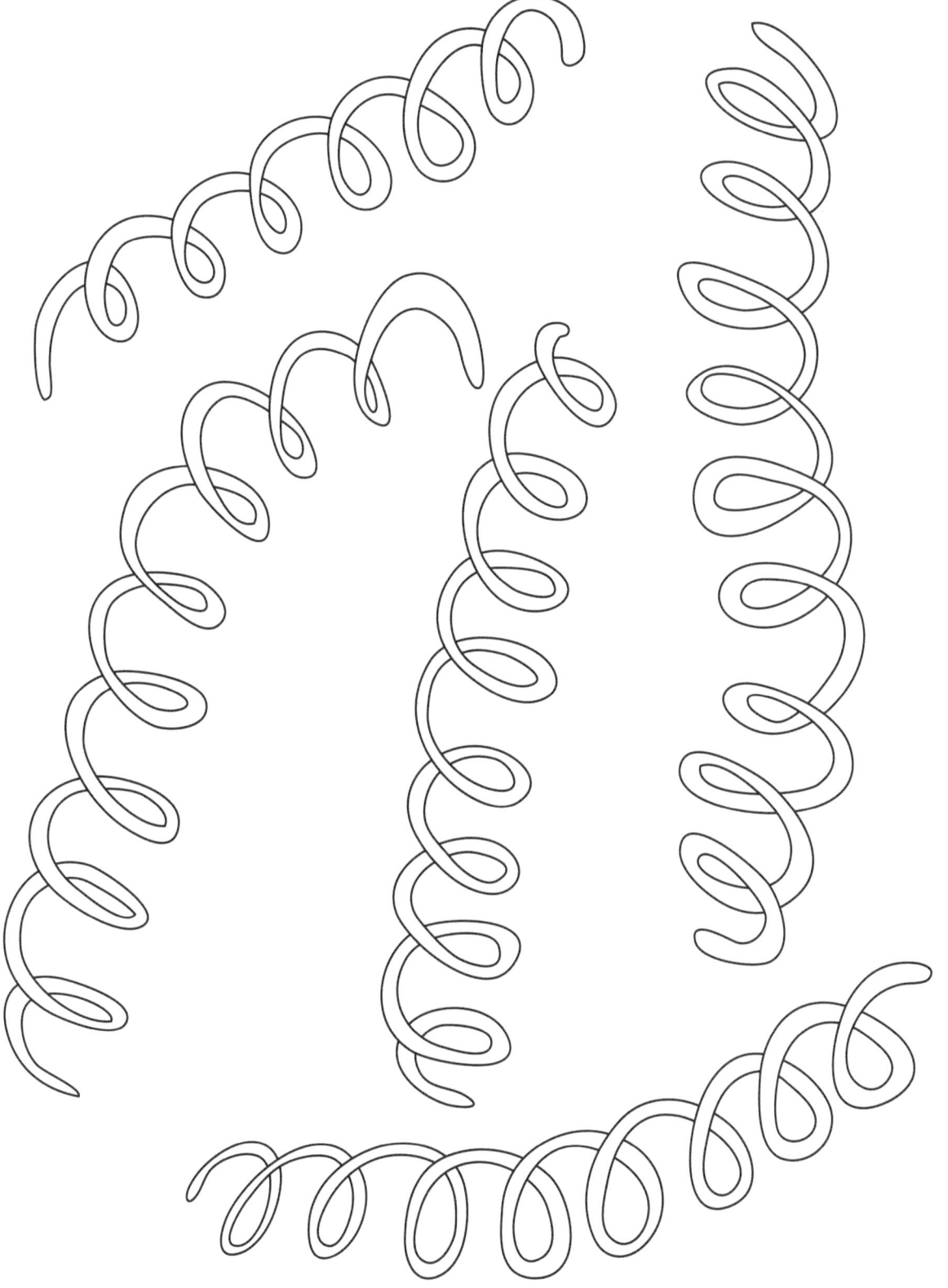

TRICHOMONIASIS➡

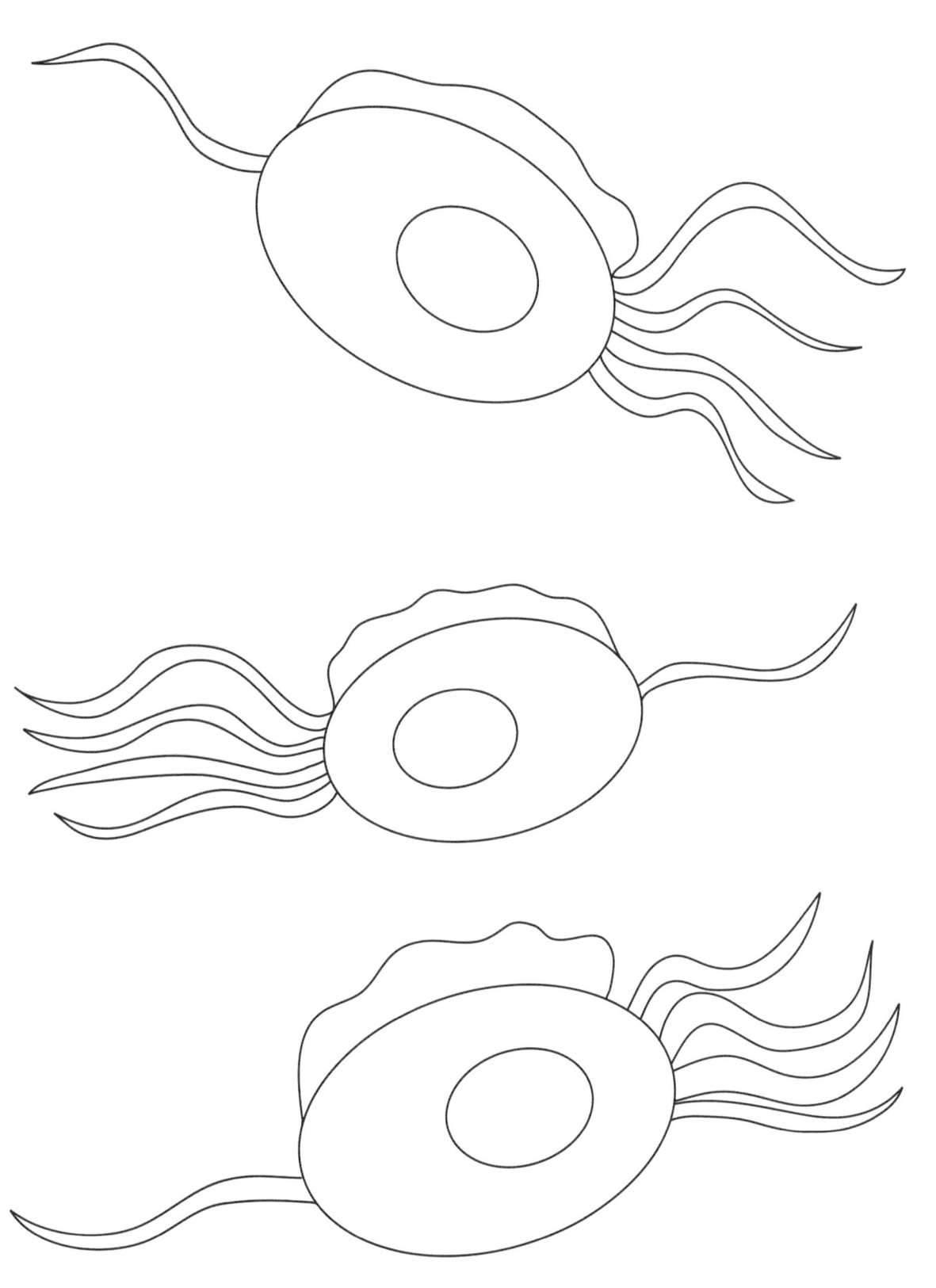

CANDIDA➡

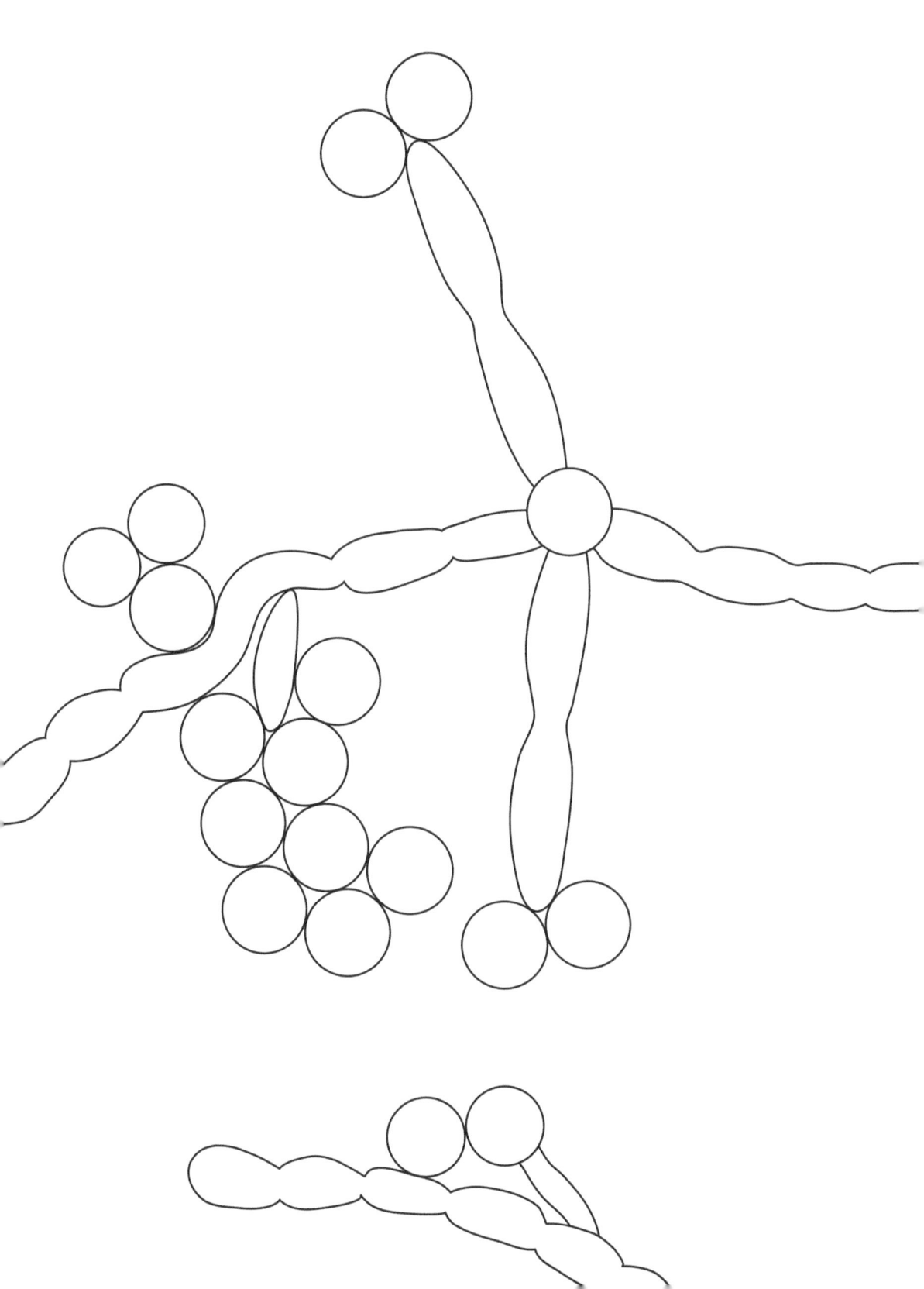

GONORRHEA➡

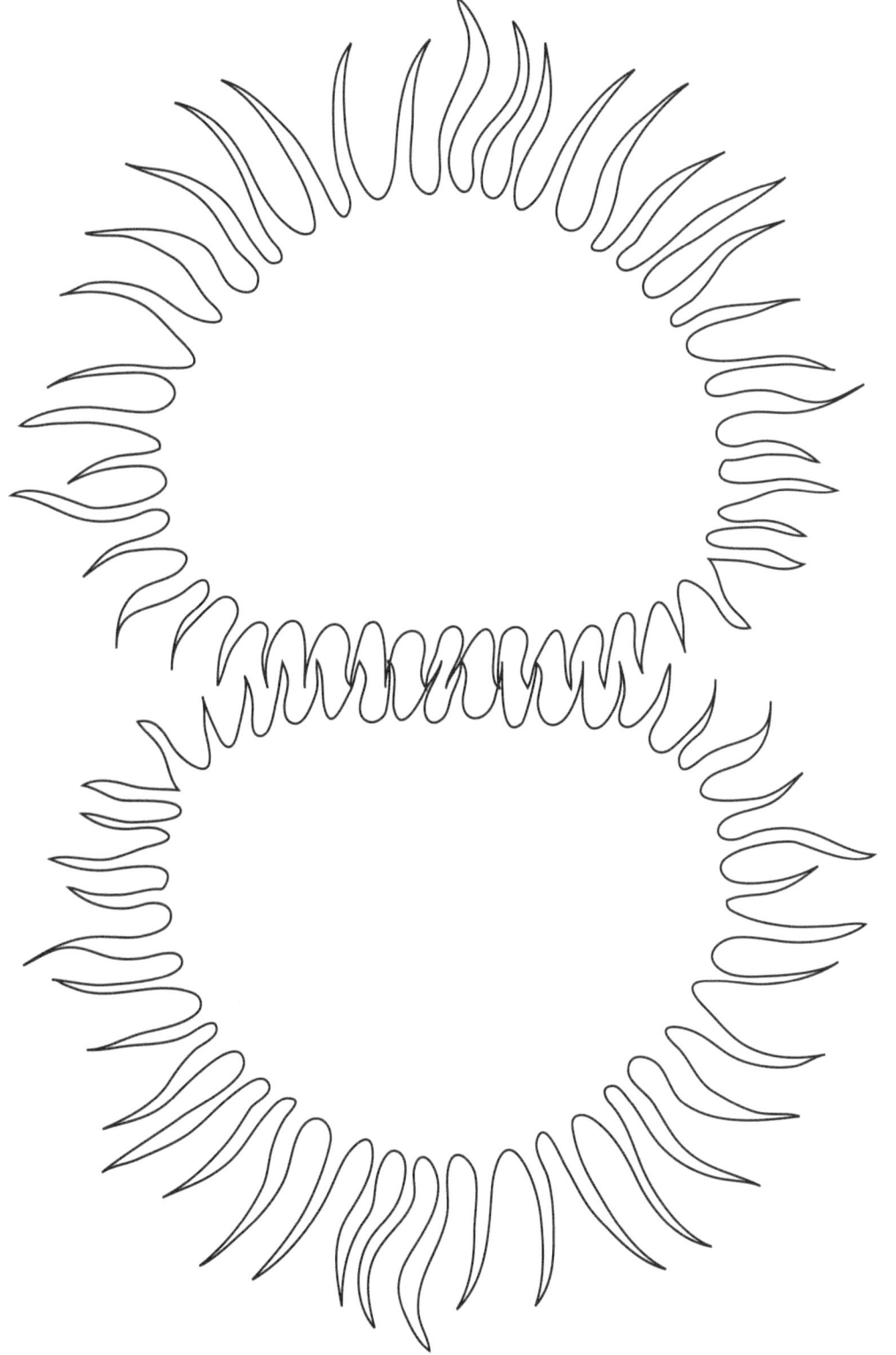

CHLAMYDIA➡

HEPATITIS B➡

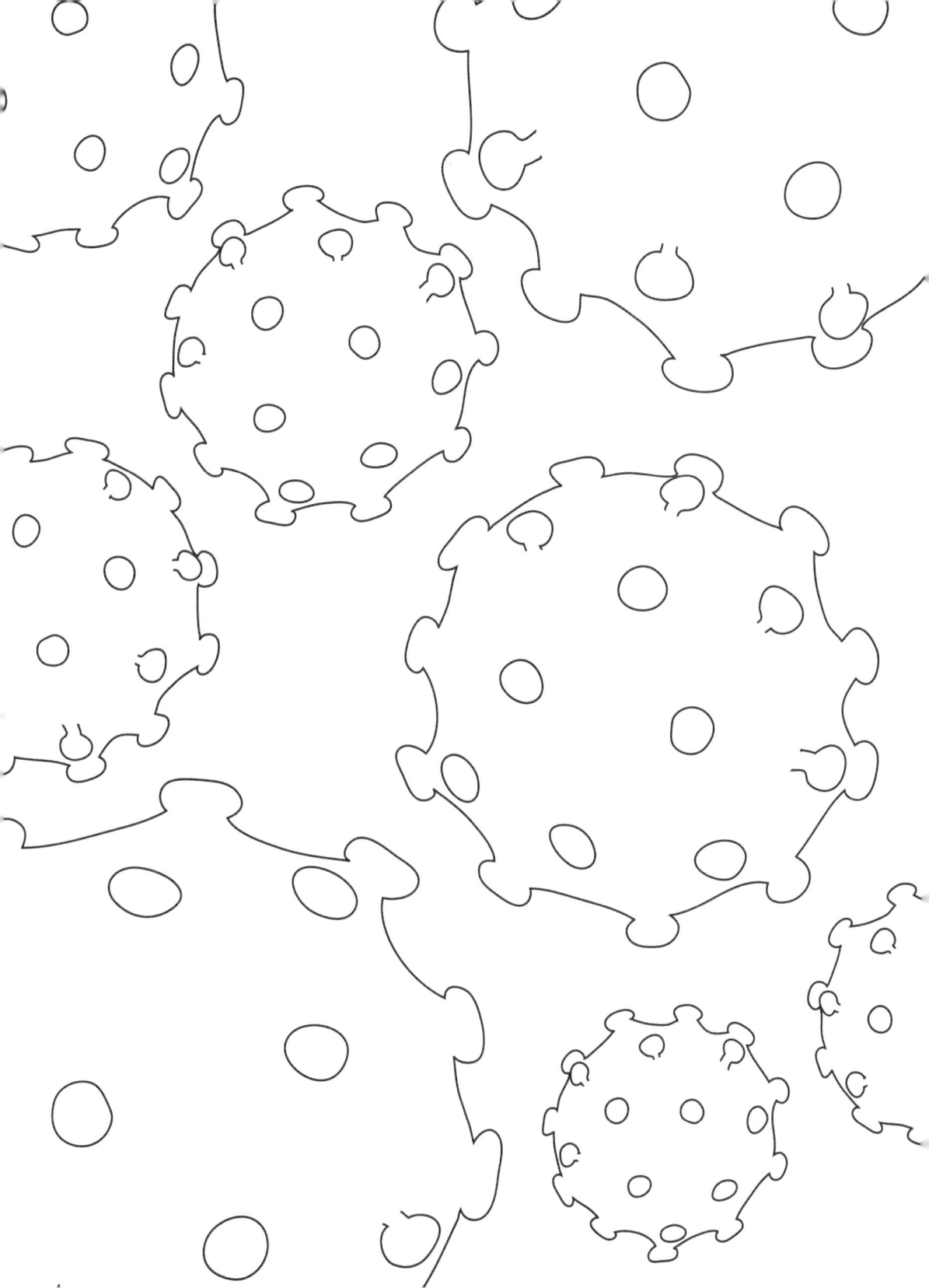

HERPES➡

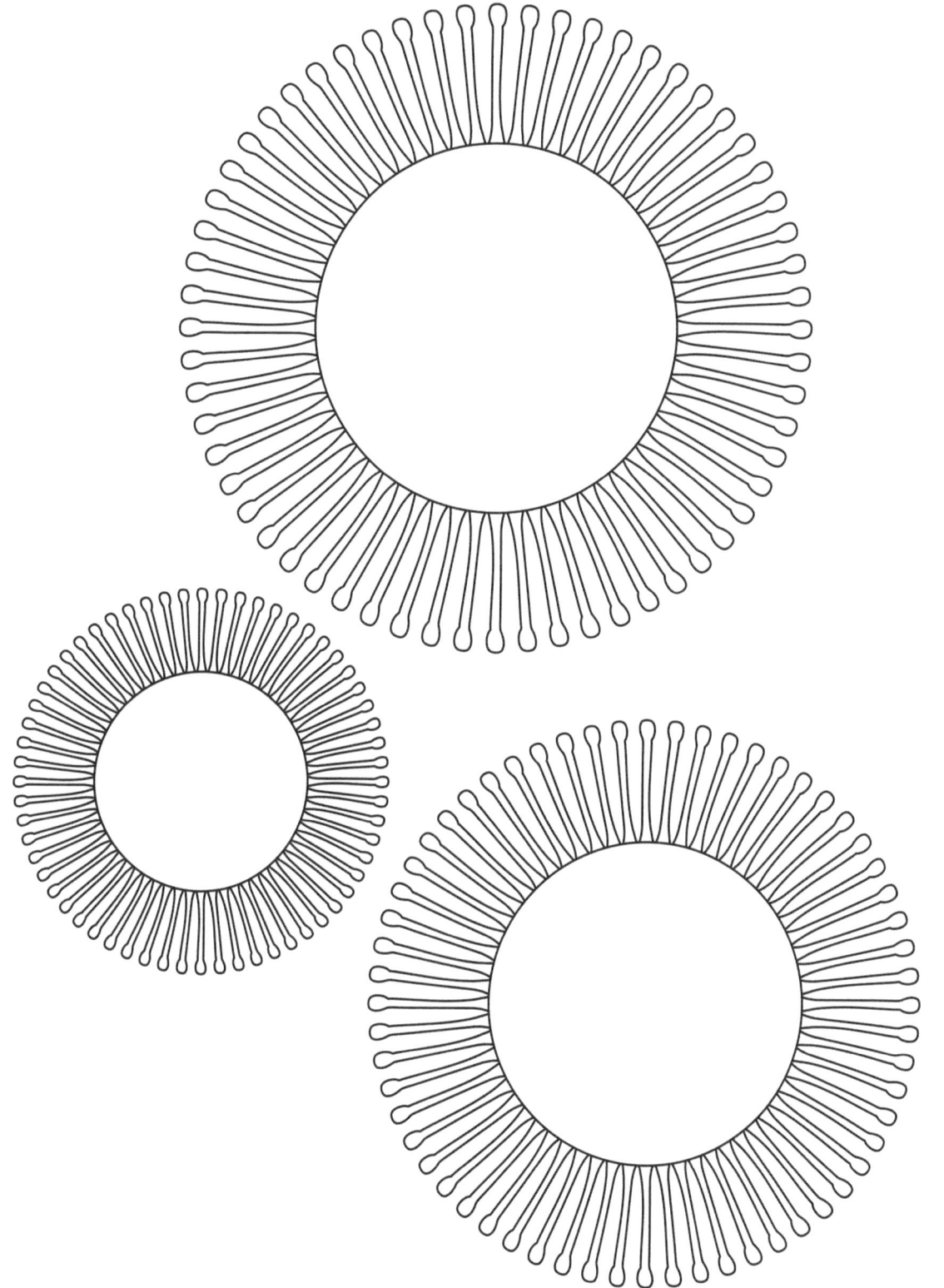

HIV➡

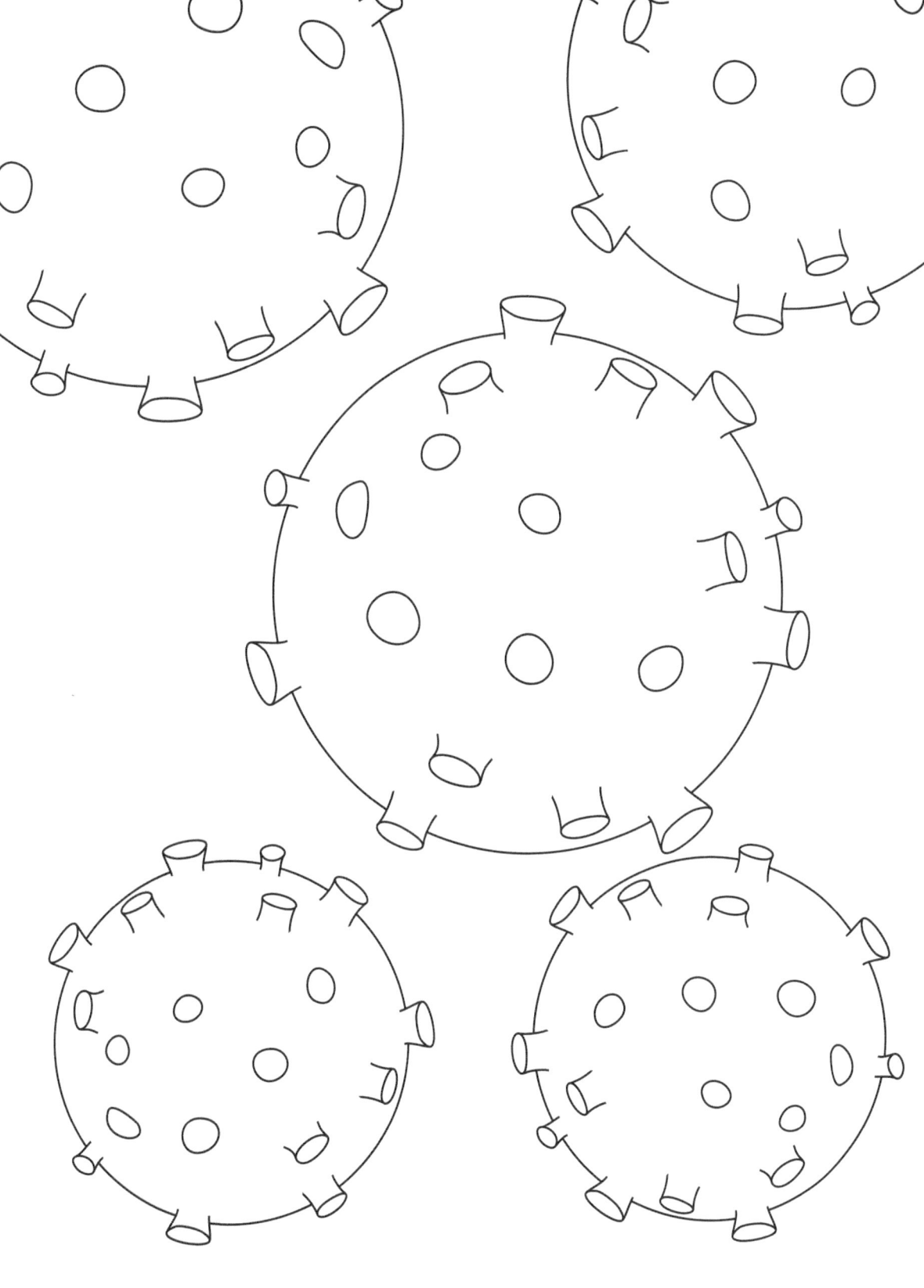

GONORRHEA➡

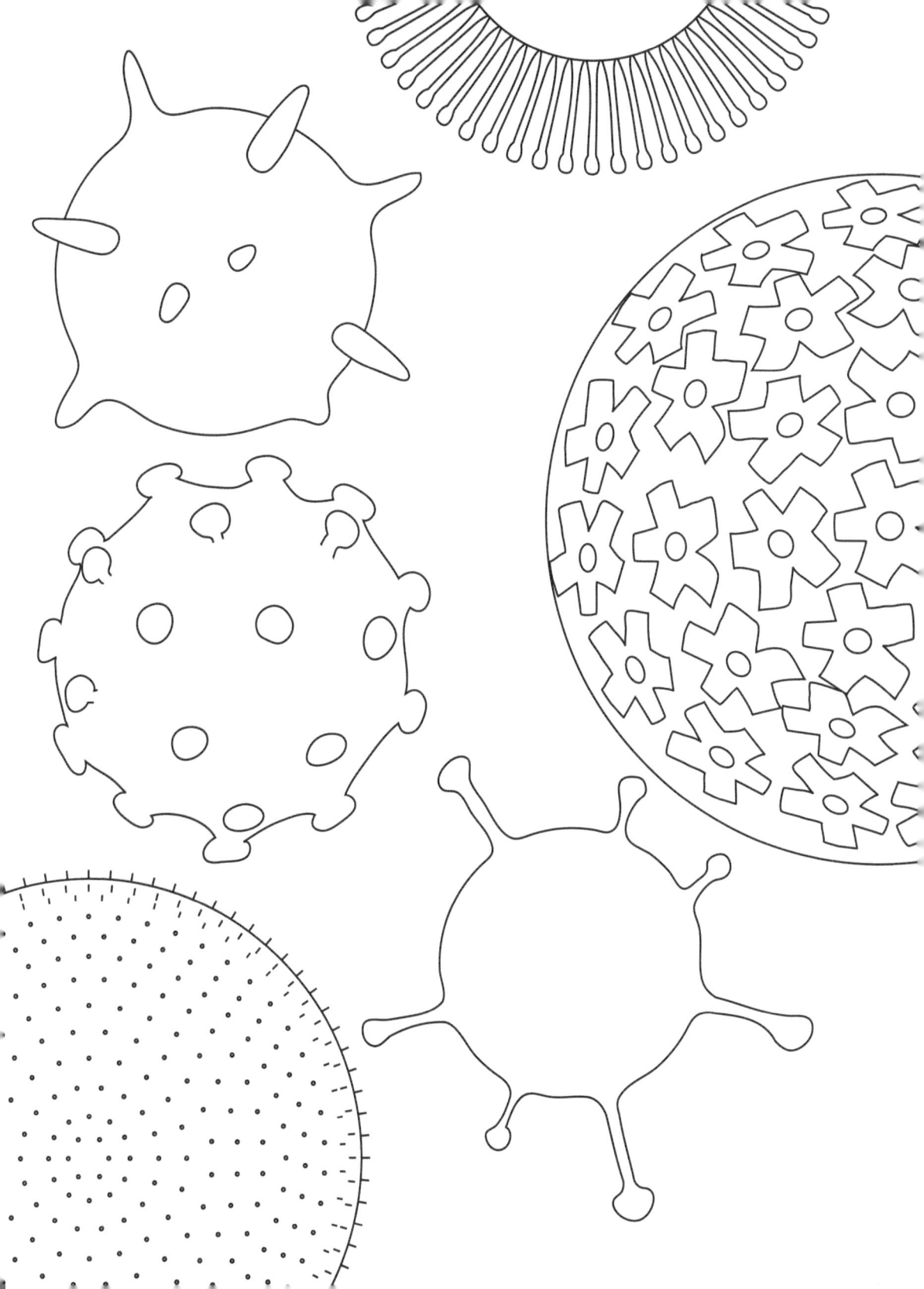